WG

# Sisters Are Forever

# Sisters Are Forever

*A Celebration of Sisterly Love & Laughter*

*by Angela Beasley Freeman*

WALNUT GROVE PRESS
Nashville, TN 37211

ISBN 1-58334-041-6

*The ideas expressed in this book are not, in all cases, exact quotations, as some have been edited for clarity and brevity. In all cases, the author has attempted to maintain the speaker's original intent. In some cases, material for this book was obtained from secondary sources, primarily print media. While every effort was made to ensure the accuracy of these sources, the accuracy cannot be guaranteed. For additions, deletions, corrections or clarifications in future editions of this text, please write WALNUT GROVE PRESS.*

Printed in the United States of America
Cover Design by Bart Dawson
Typesetting & Page Layout by Sue Gerdes
Editing by Alan Ross
1 2 3 4 5 6 7 8 9 10 • 99 00 01 02 03

ACKNOWLEDGMENTS
The author gratefully acknowledges the loving support of Carlisle & Claudette Beasley, Criswell Freeman, and Dick & Mary Freeman and gives special thanks to everyone at Walnut Grove Press.

*For my lifelong friend, mentor, and sister,*

June B. Fleming

# Table of Contents

# Introduction

A sister often doubles as a friend, a mother, a child, a peer, a rival, or some combination thereof. Whether big, little, or in between, a sister gains her position in the family. From babysitter to babysittee, from overseer to overseen, every sister has her role. Although a sister's job-description may change over the years, in the end, the career of being a sister pays the supreme dividend — a lifelong companion.

Sisters naturally have much in common, even though each develops her unique personality. In my case, my sister was older, wiser, and funnier: She was an excellent boss, and I enjoyed being her underling. When I think of the pitfalls that my sister pulled me from and the disasters she helped me detour, I thank God she held higher rank.

Certainly, you have your sisterly stories, as well. Regardless of whether you are half-sisters, stepsisters, sorority sisters, or just feel as close as sisters, this collection of quotations pays tribute to the wonderful experience of sisterhood. This book honors the fun, the struggles, and the rewards of life's everlasting blessing, a loving sister.

# 1

## *Sticking Together*

Throughout life, sisters provide each other reassurance and comfort, because they instinctively understand one another better than anyone else. While friends may come and go, sisters are a permanent part of life's landscape. Perhaps that's why sisterly alliances are strengthened during times of hardship. Simply put, sisters manage to stick together.

Shakespeare wrote, "A ministering angel shall my sister be...." On the following pages, we celebrate the faithful females who mysteriously appear as our ministering angels whenever we need them most.

There is no friend
like a sister, in calm
or stormy weather.

*Christina Rossetti*

Sisters shield us
from life's cruel circumstances.

*Nancy Mitford*

I feel about my sisters the way a mother feels
about her children…like a momma lion.

*Barbara Mandrell*

Whatever happens, I know my sisters
are there for me.

*Patti LaBelle*

My sister is laughter, even on the cloudy days of life.

*Lillian Gish*

Alone we can do so little.
Together we can do
so much.

*Helen Keller*

It's not the load that breaks you down,
it's the way you carry it.

*Lena Horne*

There are years that ask questions and years
that give answers.

*Zora Neale Hurston*

My sisters can always say or do just the
right things to make me feel better.

*Barbara Mandrell*

Women whose eyes have been washed clear
with tears get broad vision; that makes
them little sisters to all the world.

*Dorothy Dix*

A loyal sister is worth
a thousand friends.

*Marian Eigerman*

Surround yourself with
people who lift you higher.

*Oprah Winfrey*

Trouble is part of your life. And, if you don't share it, you don't give the people who love you a chance to love you enough.

*Dinah Shore*

If I can stop one heart from breaking, I shall not live in vain.

*Emily Dickinson*

We want people to feel with us more than to act for us.

*George Eliot*

$M$y sister and I had violent fights
and a fierce, blind devotion to each other.
*Helen Reddy*

$S$ome sisters never move beyond their
childhood rivalry. Most, however, develop an
affectionate attachment, a critical support
system in their middle and later years.
*Carol Saline*

$S$isters, while they are growing up,
tend to be rivals...but as they grow older,
sisters grow closer together.
*Margaret Mead*

A woman softens her own
troubles by generously
solacing those of others.

*Françoise D'Aubegne Maintenon*

Helping one another
is part of the religion
of our sisterhood.

*Louisa May Alcott*

Blessed is the influence of one true, loving
human soul upon another.

*George Eliot*

Love comforteth like sunshine after rain.

*William Shakespeare*

Few delights can equal the mere presence
of one whom we trust utterly.

*George McDonald*

Sweet is the voice of a sister in the season
of sorrow, and wise is the counsel of those
who love us.

*Benjamin Disraeli*

No matter how infrequently sisters may see each other, when the chips are really down, the sisters' bond comes into its own once again.

*Brigid McConville*

Is there any solace more
comforting than the arms
of a sister?

*Alice Walker*

Remember you are always
in the heart — tucked so
close there is no chance of
escape — of your sister.

*Katherine Mansfield*

# 2

## *Sharing*

A sister innately senses when it is time to stop and listen to another sister. Whether the talk is trivial, profound, or ridiculous, a loving sister does not judge but instead offers soothing hope and encouragement. Fortunately, a secret is safe with a sister. In spite of embarrassing or intimate discussion, sisters have the uncanny knack for putting each other at ease.

Thankfully, sisters of all ages — even if temporarily grown apart — can initiate communication at any time. Emily Dickinson writes, "I would like more sisters, so that the talking out of one's self might not leave such stillness." If you owe a sister a call, a letter, or a hug, make haste and watch stillness give way to a reassuring response.

My sister never judges
me. She's my best friend
and the only person I know
I can tell anything to.

*Lorna Luft*

Sisters share a profound bond that seems
to defy explanation.

*Arlene F. Benedict*

Listening, not imitation, is the sincerest form
of flattery.

*Dr. Joyce Brothers*

You can't fake listening. It shows.

*Raquel Welch*

The human heart, at whatever age, opens to
the heart that opens in return.

*Maria Edgeworth*

It takes a lot of courage
to show your dreams
to someone else.

*Erma Bombeck*

D istant or apart, sisters tune into each other
with an uncanniness that baffles outsiders.
*Barbara Mathias*

M eeting your sister means coming face-to-face
with your former self that still lives in her memory.
*Brigid McConville*

A squabbling resulted from sharing a bed for so
many years…we usually made a "frontier" with the
sheet folds carefully separating our domains.
*Alva Myrdal*

W hen we were thirteen, our parents got us twin
beds. But, we put a violin case in her bed, covered
it up, and the two of us slept in mine. By fifteen,
it got doggone crowded in there.
*Abigail Van Buren*
*of her sister Ann Landers*

We shared Parents.
Home. Pets. Celebrations.
Catastrophes. Secrets.
We are linked.

*Pam Brown*

$M$y sister and I slept in the same bed, and she always woke me up when she came in from a date. We'd lie there and whisper and giggle. I wanted to be just like her.

*Minnie Pearl,*
*of her sister*

$L$ast night Margot and I were lying side by side in my bed. It was incredibly cramped, but that's what made it fun.

*Anne Frank,*
*of her sister*

$S$isters, whatever their stories, instinctively know how fortunate they are.

*Susan Ripps*

Knowing a sister is like having a sixth-sense
perception of someone.

*Brigid McConville*

Sisters — as youngsters they may share
popsicles, chewing gum, hair dryers and
bedrooms. When they grow up, they share
confidences, careers, children, and chats.

*Roxanne Brown*

Sisters who have learned
to share as children may
go on sharing for the rest
of their lives.

*Brigid McConville*

$S$haring is sometimes more demanding
than giving.

*Mary Catherine Bateson*

$O$ne of the best things about being an adult
is the realization that you can share with your
sister and still have plenty left for yourself.

*Betsy Cohen*

While some sisters
are kindred spirits from
the very beginning, I really
began to appreciate
my sister years later.

*Alda Ellis*

When my sister and I talked together, the words had meaning yet did not weigh too heavily upon us.

*Simone de Beauvoir*

I once asked Margot if she thought I was ugly.
She said that I was cute and had nice eyes.
A little vague, don't you think?

*Anne Frank*

Each family of sisters has a language
and a turn of phrase all its own.

*Barbara Mathias*

I should love her even if
she were not my sister;
and even if she
did not love me.

*Elizabeth Barrett Browning*

# 3

## *Lessons*

An important aspect of sisterhood is teaching. In the early years, big sisters dispense important information about everything from babysitting to boys. In time, younger sisters also have much to teach — although senior siblings sometimes ignore the lessons. By adulthood, a sister often becomes a masterful mentor who takes time to listen, encourage, and motivate. For some reliable instruction from sisters of all ages, read on...

We can learn something new any time
that we believe we can.

*Virginia Satir*

Nothing in life is to be feared.
It is only to be understood.

*Marie Curie*

Water finds its level, and children learn.

*Leo Tolstoy*

Everywhere, we learn from those we love.

*Goethe*

What is a sister?
She is your teacher,
your defense attorney,
even your shrink.

*Barbara Alpert*

Sisters serve as teachers, role models,
problem- solvers, confidantes, challengers,
socializers, protectors, and caregivers.

*Dale V. Atkins*

Sisters fundamentally shape
the kind of people we become.

*Brigid McConville*

I watched every move my older sister Dixie
made. I couldn't wait to grow up
so that I could be like her.

*Minnie Pearl*

Many years later, Madge had only to use
the elder sister voice, and I would feel
chills down my spine.

*Agatha Christie*

I wanted to give my
younger sisters everything
I had missed.

*Margaret Mead*

Everybody must learn this lesson somewhere
— it costs something to be what you are.
*Shirley Abbot*

Example is the school of humankind,
and they will learn at no other.
*Edmund Burke*

Teachers teach more by what they are
than by what they say.
*Anonymous*

My sister showed me what was possible.

*Lynn Redgrave*

Nothing is so infectious as example.

*La Rochefoucauld*

Teaching my sister to read, write, and count gave me, from the age of six onward, a sense of pride in my own efficacy...I felt I was at last creating something real.

*Simone de Beauvoir*

Learning is not attained by chance.
It must be sought with ardor and
attended with diligence.

*Abigail Adams*

With a sister, you learn to love and to argue,
to share and to spat.

*Dale V. Atkins*

If you can't be a good
example, then you'll just have
to be a horrible warning.

*Catherine Aird*

While we teach, we learn.

*Seneca*

In time, we grow to trust the future
for our answers.

*Ruth Benedict*

Learning without wisdom is a load of books
on a donkey's back.

*Zora Neale Hurston*

In youth we learn; in age
we understand.

*Marie von Ebner-Eschenbach*

We are each other's reference points
at our turning points.

*Elizabeth Fishel*

Families the world around are the place
where people learn who they are
and how to be that way.

*Jean Illsley Clarke*

There are some things you learn best in calm,
some in storm.

*Willa Cather*

There are no mistakes,
no coincidences; all events
are blessings given to us
to learn from.

*Elisabeth Kübler-Ross*

My sister taught me
everything I needed to
know, and she was only
in the sixth grade
at the time.

*Linda Sunshine*

# 4

## *Forever Friends*

Sooner or later, sisters become best friends. Of course there's an occasional exception to this rule...sisters who, for reasons of personality or distance, do not make the connection. But, most sisters find themselves happily involved in an ever-deepening friendship that grows richer with each passing year.

Tracy Chapman says, "My sister is my best critic, my best audience, and my best friend." Typically, these relationships grow even stronger through the years. Yes, the test of time proves that sisters really are a girl's best friend...with apologies to canines everywhere.

A friend you might have to give up. But, you can't give up a sister. You were born with her, and you die with her.

*Elizabeth Mead Steig*

Over the years, sisters generally draw closer, knitting together their defenses out of common threads.

*Elizabeth Fishel*

Now that I am an adult, my siblings are even more important: we age together.

*Jane Mersky Leder*

Best friend, my wellspring in the wilderness....

*George Eliot*

If Sadie is molasses,
then I'm vinegar. Sadie is
sugar and I'm spice…but
we were best friends
from day one.

*Bessie Delany*

To have a loving relationship with a sister is
not simply to have a buddy or a confidante —
it is to have a soulmate for life.

*Victoria Secunda*

The sister relationship parallels friendship,
but additional dynamics are at work.

*Dee Brestin*

The bond between sisters is unique, stretching
and bending through periods of closeness
and distance, but almost never breaking.

*Carol Saline*

Our relationship was as simple as breath, as complex as circulation.

*Elizabeth Fishel*

# It is better to make one's friendships at home.

*Plutarch*

The growth of true
friendship may be
a lifelong affair.

*Sarah Orne Jewett*

We were friends throughout life with that
intimacy but also — as children —
with that squabbling.

*Alva Myrdal*

A faithful friend is a strong defense.

*Louisa May Alcott*

The tie of a sister is near and dear indeed.

*Charlotte Brontë*

My sister is the friend who shows me
what I want from other friends.

*Michele D' Ambrosio*

Friendship is the bread of the heart.

*Mary Russell Mitford*

The best thing about having a sister is that
you always have a friend.

*Cali Rae Turner*

For better or worse, sisters remain sisters,
until death do they part.

*Brigid McConville*

Having a sister is like having a best friend
that you can't get rid of. You know whatever
you do, she'll still be there.

*Amy Li*

To throw away an honest friend is
to throw your life away.

*Sophocles*

Even after death, the language
of sisters endures.

*Elizabeth Fishel*

Hold a true friend with both hands.

*Nigerian Proverb*

Friendship: one soul in two bodies.

*Pythagoras*

A friend is a second self.

*Cicero*

Sisterhood is a club with
a lifetime membership.

*Karen Brown*

Friends may come and friends may go, but a sister remains forever.

*Arlene F. Benedict*

# 5

## *Life*

Sisters share their victories and comfort each other through life's disappointments. A caring, loving sister — biological or otherwise — enriches us as we change and grow. As Anne Morrow Lindbergh observes, "There is more life where my sister is." To get the most out of your life, find your sister…fast! Life awaits and so does she.

*Life*

Life is a succession of readjustments.

*Elizabeth Bowen*


Life is change; growth is optional.

*Karen Kaiser Clark*


Life goes on, having nowhere else to go.

*Diane Ackerman*


I want a busy life, a just mind,
and a timely death.

*Zora Neale Hurston*

Life begins when a person
first realizes how soon
it ends.

*Marcelene Cox*

There is no good reason why we should not develop and change until the last day we live.

*Karen Horney*

Only I can change my life.
No one can do it for me.

*Carol Burnett*

You've got to keep growing or you're just like last night's cornbread: stale and dry.

*Loretta Lynn*

All our lives, we're preparing to be something or somebody, even if we don't know it.

*Katherine Anne Porter*

From birth to death, sisters model and pattern their scripts after each other. They take cues from each other about the way life is or might be.

*Elizabeth Fishel*

Many women say their lives have evolved as a pattern interwoven with their sisters'. A sister's influence may make itself felt at all levels.

*Brigid McConville*

What matters most is that we learn from living.

*Doris Lessing*

My sisters taught me how to live.

*Georgette Wasserstein*

The real trick is to stay alive as long as you live.
*Ann Landers*

Life isn't a straight line. Most of us have to be transplanted, like a tree, before we blossom.
*Louise Nevelson*

Life is creation,
self and circumstances the raw material.
*Dorothy M. Richardson*

Life is my college. May I graduate well
and earn some honors.
*Louisa May Alcott*

One is not born a woman,
one becomes one.

*Simone de Beauvoir*

Dreams pass into reality
of action. From the action
stems the dream again;
and this interdependence
produces the highest living.

*Anaïs Nin*

No life is so hard that you can't make it
easier by the way you take it.

*Ellen Glasgow*

Life is what we make it. Always has been.
Always will be.

*Grandma Moses*

Happiness is nothing but everyday living
seen through a veil.

*Zora Neale Hurston*

Courage is the price life extracts
for granting peace.

*Amelia Earhart*

I think your whole life
shows in your face…
and you should be
proud of that.

*Lauren Bacall*

Life is constructed so that the event does not, cannot, and will not match the expectation.

*Charlotte Brontë*

Life is under no obligation to give us what we expect.

*Margaret Mitchell*

We live in a fantasy world, a world of illusion. The great task in life is to find reality.

*Iris Murdoch*

Life forms illogical patterns. It is haphazard and full of beauties, which I try to catch as they fly by — for who knows whether any of them will ever return?

*Margot Fonteyn*

Her sister's parallel life is a "yardstick" or
"touchstone" — a constant point of reference
from which she can gauge her own identity.

*Brigid McConville*

Many of us have learned more about life
from our sisters than from anyone else.

*Dale V. Atkins*

Dear sister, you can't think how I depend
upon you, and when you're not there
the color goes out of my life.

*Virginia Woolf*

She could give me what no queen could give:
Keys to the secret, How to Live.

*Lucy Larcom*

Life is like a butterfly. You can chase it,
or you can let it come to you.

*Ruth Brown*

Learn to get in touch with the silence within
and know that everything in life has a purpose.

*Elisabeth Kübler-Ross*

One of the goals in life is to try and be in
touch with one's most personal themes —
the values, ideas, styles, colors that are the
touchstones of one's individual life,
its real texture and substance.

*Gloria Vanderbilt*

Life has no blessing quite like a loving sister
who understands you.

*Janet Lanese*

How lucky we are
to have a sister with us
on the journey of life.

*Arlene F. Benedict*

# 6

## *Family*

No matter how great the difference in their ages, sisters share permanent familial ties. This bond may, for various reasons, be tested to the limit but will never break. Ariel and Will Durant write, "The family is the nucleus of civilization." From the relative security of this nurturing nucleus, sisters eventually venture out from the family in order to experience the ups and downs of life on their own. Yet, no matter how far she strays, the welcome mat back home will always greet a loving sister.

Call it a clan, a network, a tribe,or a family.
Whatever you call it, you need it.

*Jane Howard*

From birth to death, the sibling relationship
undergoes an amazing amount of change and
development all because the players involved
continue to evolve and grow.

*Susan Scarf Merrell*

Sibling relationships are often life's
longest-lasting relationships.

*Stephen P. Banks*

The family is that dear octopus from whose
tentacles we never quite escape, nor, in our
innermost hearts, ever quite wish to.

*Dodie Smith*

Family is the we of me.

*Carson McCullers*

They are a constant; they are family.
That provides comfort knowing the bonds will
survive despite the differences.

*Jane Mersky Leder*

Sisterhood is probably the most competitive
relationship within the family, but once sisters
are grown, it is the strongest relationship.

*Margaret Mead*

She rides in the front seat:
She's my older sister.

*Carly Simon*

When there's a sibling,
There's a quibbling.

*Selma Raskin*

 $S$ oup is a lot like family. Each ingredient
enhances the others; each batch has its own
characteristics; and it needs time to simmer
to reach the full flavor.

*Marge Kennedy*


 $T$ he family...We're a strange little band of
characters trudging through life sharing diseases,
toothpaste, coveting one another's desserts,
hiding shampoo, borrowing money, locking each
other out of rooms, loving, laughing, defending,
and trying to figure out the common thread
that bound us all together.

*Erma Bombeck*

Better a hundred enemies outside the house
than one inside.

*Arabian Proverb*

Keep your family from the abominable
practice of backbiting.

*The Old Farmer's Almanac, 1811*

It is a reverent thing to see an ancient castle
or building not in decay, or to see a fair timber
tree sound and perfect. How much more to
behold an ancient and noble family that has
stood against the waves and weathers of time.

*Francis Bacon*

In time of test, family is best.

*Burmese Proverb*

You leave home to seek your fortune and when you get it, you go home and share it with your family.

*Anita Baker*

Family faces are magic mirrors.
    Looking at people who belong to us,
    we see past, present, and future.
                                    *Gail Lumet Buckley*

Brothers and sisters are as close
    as hands and feet.
                                    *Vietnamese Proverb*

We four sisters were there for each other in
good times and bad, for richer and poorer, in
sickness and in health…until death do we part.
                                    *Dianne Lennon*

Family loyalties involve certain obligations.
Be cheerful. Keep things in good repair.
Keep your spirits up. Think in harmony.
Do all that, and the God of love and peace
will be with you for sure.
*2 Corinthians: 13:11*
*(The Message)*

The desire to be and have a sister is a desire
to know and be known by someone who shares
your blood and body, history and dreams....
*Elizabeth Fishel*

Children in a family are like flowers in a
bouquet: there's always one determined
to face in an opposite direction from
the way the arranger desires.

*Marcelene Cox*

A family is a unit composed not only of
children, but of men, women, an occasional
animal, and the common cold.

*Ogden Nash*

The family is one of nature's masterpieces.

*George Santayana*

Our most basic instinct is not for survival but
for family. Most of us would give our own life
for the survival of a family member; yet, we lead
our daily life too often as if we take our family
for granted.

*Paul Pearsall*

What can you do
to promote world peace?
Go home and
love your family.

*Mother Teresa*
Upon receiving the Nobel Peace Prize

You don't choose your family. They are God's gift to you, as you are to them.

*Archbishop Desmond Tutu*

Sisterhood is a sibling revelry.

*Karen Brown*

The need for family — for nurture, stability, sharing — does not stay behind when one leaves one's home.

*Karen Lindsey*

Home is where you learn values. It's the responsibility of the family.

*Melba Moore*

It takes a heap of livin' in a house
to make it home.

*Edgar A. Guest*

When you look at your life, the greatest
happiness is family happiness.

*Dr. Joyce Brothers*

Home ought to be our clearinghouse, the
place from which we go forth…ready for life.

*Kathleen Norris*

After a certain age, the more one becomes
oneself, the more obvious one's
family traits appear.

*Marcel Proust*

It has long been my belief
that in times of great
stress, such as a four-day
vacation, the thin veneer
of family wears off
almost at once, and we
are revealed in our
true personalities.

*Shirley Jackson*

# 7

## *Memories*

An old English proverb suggests, "Memories are the treasure of the mind." And what treasure is more precious than the memories of family? All sisters have a mutual heritage and history. In reliving and retelling their stories, sisters stay young at heart.

American primitive painter Grandma Moses observes, "Memory is a painter. It paints pictures of the past." Sisters can create charming portraits by recalling their countless positive adventures of childhood. By exploring the hidden trails of the past together, sisters discover invaluable buried treasures.

Our brothers and sisters
are there for us from
the dawn of our
personal stories to
the inevitable dusk.

*Susan Scarf Merrell*

Memory is the diary we all carry within us.

*Mary H. Waldrip*

Childhood memories live beneath the surface
of a sister's mind, never quite forgotten and
long since incorporated into a sense of
her sibling and herself.

*Brigid McConville*

There is no one else on earth with whom you
share so much personal history.

*Judith Viorst*

It suddenly became clear to me that my sister
was the one person who had known me
for the longest time.

*Elizabeth Jolley*

What sets sisters apart from brothers —
and also from friends — is a very intimate
meshing of the heart, the soul, and
the mystical cords of memory.

*Carol Saline*

Sisters share a mutual knowledge
of the intuitive and unspoken.

*Brigid McConville*

Friends can be close, but none so close as one
who shares your history, lineage, and legacy.

*Alda Ellis*

What greater thing is
there for human souls than
to feel that they are joined
for life — to be with
each other in silent,
unspoken memories.

*George Eliot*

Our siblings are the only people who can
truly share all of our happy and unhappy
childhood memories with us.

*Susan Scarf Merrell*

There are so many memories…the interweaving
of those joyful, angry, painful, and historic
memories which create the foundation
for every sister-relationship.

*Carol Saline*

Often in old age, sisters become each other's
chosen companions. In addition to shared
memories of childhood…they share memories of
the same home, the same homemaking style, and
the small prejudices about housekeeping that
carry the echoes of their mother's voice.

*Margaret Mead*

No one knows better than a sister how we
grew up and who were our favorite friends,
teachers and toys.

*Dale V. Atkins*

Our siblings push buttons that can cast us
back into the roles we felt sure we'd let go of
long ago — the baby, the peacekeeper, the
caretaker….It doesn't seem to matter
how much time has elapsed or
how far we've traveled.

*Jane Mersky Leder*

God gave us memories so that we might
have roses in December.

*James M. Barrie*

Lord, keep my memory green.

*Charles Dickens*

As siblings we were inextricably bound....
No matter how old we got or how often we
tried to show another face, reality was filtered
through yesterday's memories.

*Jane Mersky Leder*

May I forget what ought to be forgotten and
recall unfailingly all that ought to be recalled.

*Laura Palmer*

A retentive memory is a good thing, but the ability to forget is the true token of greatness.

*Elbert Hubbard*

S ome memories are better than anything that can ever happen to one again.

*Willa Cather*

T o be able to enjoy one's past is to be able to live twice.

*Martial*

O ne's sister is a part of one's essential self, an eternal presence of one's heart and soul and memory.

*Susan Cahill*

We wove a web in childhood,
      A web of sunny air.

*Charlotte Brontë*

Blessed be childhood, which brings down
      something of heaven into the midst of
            our rough earthliness.

*Henri Frédéric Amiel*

The events of childhood do not pass, but
      repeat themselves like seasons of the year.

*Eleanor Farjeon*

What we remember from childhood we
      remember forever — permanent ghosts,
            stamped, imprinted, eternally seen.

*Cynthia Ozick*

Bliss in possession
will not last,
Remembered joys
are never past.

*James Montgomery*

The hills of one's youth
are all mountains.

*Mari Sandez*

# 8

## *Sisterly Advice*

How is it that a sister never runs short of advice? When asked, sisters can counsel us on every aspect of life, love, and happiness. But, savvy sisters know that giving opinions also carries with it responsibility. As Flannery O'Connor writes, "I am very handy with my advice and when anybody appears to be following it, I get frantic!" For tips on living frantic-free, flip the page…

The true secret of giving advice is, after you've honestly given it, to be perfectly indifferent whether it is taken or not.

*Hannah Whitall Smith*

It is very difficult to live among people you love and hold back from offering them advice.

*Anne Tyler*

Your sister believes you are wise, especially when you come to her for advice.

*Karen Brown*

Advice is what we ask for when we already
know the answer but wish we didn't.

*Erica Jong*

Please give me some good advice in your
next letter. I promise not to follow it.

*Edna St. Vincent Millay*

It is not enough to reach for the brass ring.
You must also enjoy the merry-go-round.

*Julie Andrews*

We carry the seeds of happiness
wherever we go.

*Martha Washington*

This is happiness: to be dissolved in something
complete and great.

*Willa Cather*

Noble deeds and hot baths are the best cure
for sadness.

*Dodie Smith*

Until it has loved, no man or woman
can become itself.

*Emily Dickinson*

There is a net of love by which
you can catch souls.

*Mother Teresa*

There is always something left to love.
If you haven't learned that,
you haven't learned anything.

*Lorraine Hansberry*

I have found this paradox: If I love until it
hurts, then there is no hurt but only more love.

*Mother Teresa*

You'll never do a whole lot unless you're
brave enough to try.

*Dolly Parton*

You may be disappointed if you fail,
but you are doomed if you don't try.

*Beverly Sills*

A ship in port is safe, but that's not
what ships are built for.

*Grace Murray Hopper*

You will do foolish things,
but do them with enthusiasm.

*Colette*

To love what you do and feel that it matters
— how could anything be more fun?

*Katharine Graham*

Risk! Risk anything! Care no more for the
opinions of others. Do the hardest thing on
earth. Act for yourself. Face the truth.

*Katherine Mansfield*

You are unique, and, if that is not fulfilled,
something has been lost.

*Martha Graham*

The first and worst of all frauds is to cheat
one's self. All sin is easy after that.

*Pearl Bailey*

The downhill path is easy,
    but it's hard to turn back.

*Christina Rossetti*

A ruffled mind makes a restless pillow.

*Charlotte Brontë*

You must learn to be still in the midst of
    activity and to be vibrantly alive in repose.

*Indira Gandhi*

Follow your instincts. That's where true wisdom
    manifests itself.

*Oprah Winfrey*

If you listen to your conscience, it will serve you as no other friend you've ever known.

*Loretta Young*

I think all great innovations
            are built on rejection.

*Louise Nevelson*

There is nothing final about a mistake,
            except its being taken as final.

*Phyllis Bottome*

Considering how dangerous everything is,
            nothing is really frightening.

*Gertrude Stein*

Success is achieved by those who do not know
            that failure is inevitable.

*Coco Chanel*

Fail forwards toward success.

*Mary Kay Ash*

Faith can put a candle in the darkest night.
*Margaret Sangster*

Without faith, nothing is possible.
With it, nothing is impossible.
*Mary McLeod Bethune*

Believe in something larger than yourself.
*Barbara Bush*

Before your dreams can come true,
you need to have those dreams.
*Dr. Joyce Brothers*

When you have a dream, you've got to
grab it and never let go.
*Carol Burnett*

People who fight fire with fire usually end up
with ashes.

*Abigail Van Buren*

Jealousy is the most dreadfully involuntary
of all sins.

*Iris Murdoch*

There is nothing that makes you like
other human beings so much
as doing things for them.

*Zora Neale Hurston*

Let us make one point...that we meet each
other with a smile...smile at each other,
make time for each other in your family.

*Mother Teresa*

Treat your friends like family and your family
like friends.

*Michele Slung*

Live each day as it comes, and don't borrow
trouble by worrying about tomorrow.

*Dorothy Dix*

Leave the table while you still feel that
you could eat a little more.

*Helena Rubinstein*

Laugh at yourself first,
    before anyone else can.

*Elsa Maxwell*

It took me a long time not to judge myself
    through someone else's eyes.

*Sally Field*

Love yourself first.

*Lucille Ball*

Trust your hunches....Hunches are usually
based on facts filed away below the conscious.
    But be warned: Don't confuse hunches
        with wishful thinking.

*Dr. Joyce Brothers*

The ultimate in being successful is the luxury of giving yourself the time to do what you want to do.

*Leontyne Price*

It is never too late to be
what you might have been.

*George Eliot*

# 9

## *A Sister Is...*

A sister is a bundle of blessings, bound by love and laughter. A mix of intimacy, competition, caring, and time help create the unbreakable bond of sisterhood — a lifelong connection, a kinship enduring from the cradle to the grave.

Writer Charlotte Brontë speaks to the unique qualities of sisterhood when writing, "You know as well as I do the value of sisters' affections for each other; there is nothing like it in the world." If you are blessed with a loving sister, give thanks for your gift of unending love that is truly like nothing else in the world.

Your sister is your other self. She's your alter ego, your reflection, your foil, your shadow.

*Barbara Mathias*

A sister is both your mirror —
and your opposite.

*Elizabeth Fishel*

What is a sister? She is your mirror, shining back at you with a world of possibilities.

*Barbara Alpert*

Now that I am without
your company, I feel not
only that I am deprived of
a very dear sister, but that
I have lost half of myself.

*Beatrice D'Este*

My sister was the first
person I could tell
the truth to.

*Elizabeth Fishel*

A sister is a friend — someone we grew up
with, fought with, and learned from.

*Arlene F. Benedict*

From the early years of life, the sisters'
relationship is one of the most emotionally
charged of all relationships.

*Dale V. Atkins*

A sister can be seen as someone who is
both ourselves and very much not ourselves —
a special kind of double.

*Toni Morrison*

Every woman is like — yet unlike —
her sister.

*Brigid McConville*

A woman's best support
is a dear sister.

*Helen Stewart*

A sister is often the person who understands you best.

*Janet Lanese*

It is in coming to terms with the sense
of being the same and different which is
at the heart of the sister's relationship.
*Brigid McConville*

The pull between sisters is the realization
of similarity versus the need for difference.
*Elizabeth Fishel*

.

To know a sister is to know a paradox.

*Patricia Foster*

Sisters are our peers, the voice of our times.

*Elizabeth Fishel*

Sisterhood is
a lifelong conversation.

*Karen Brown*

After so long together,
my sister and I are,
in some ways,
like one person.

*Sadie Delany*

My sister's presence
makes the room feel
warm and alive.

*Anne Morrow Lindbergh*

I recognize how crucial
my relationship with my
sister is in defining myself.

*Barbara Mathias*

Of all the people, my sister's stamp of approval
was most important because she knew me
better than anyone.

*Ann Kiemel*

Both within the family and without, our sisters
hold up images of who we are and
who we can dare to become.

*Elizabeth Fishel*

Sisters are girlfriends, rivals, listening-posts, shopping buddies, confidantes, and much, much more.

*Carol Saline*

I realize how sweet and slippery is the word "sister" — big enough to stretch beyond biology and across time; flexible enough for soulmates and virtual strangers; precise enough to embrace me and my two sisters, my two daughters, and all the sisterhoods in between.

*Letty Cottin Pogrebin*

# We are sisters.
# We will always be sisters.

*Nancy Kelton*

# 10

## *Observations*

We conclude with a few congenial observations concerning sisterhood. Enjoy. And when you're done, why not pick up the phone and give your sister a call?

Although as an adult, you and your sister
may live in very different worlds, you share the
source from which you learned about life.

*Dale V. Atkins*

Sisters are connected throughout their lives
by a special bond — whether they try
to ignore it or not.

*Brigid McConville*

Having a sister means having one of the most
beautiful and unique of human relationships.

*Robert Strand*

I am very lucky.
I don't have a husband,
but I do have a sister.

*Coretta Scott King*

Living with a sister
is easier than moving in
with a friend.

*Jeanie Pyun*

Bessie and I probably
know each other
better than any two
human beings on earth.

*Sadie Delany*

Sisters define their rivalry in terms
        of competition for the golden cup
            of parental love.

*Elizabeth Fishel*

Adult sisters who still compete for the
        limelight will have a difficult time.

*Dale V. Atkins*

It occurs to me that one can never fully
        grow up with one's sister. In some secret
        place, we always remain seven and eight.

*Patricia Foster*

There is a place within sisterhood for likeness and difference, for those subtle differences that challenge and delight.

*Christine Downing*

There is no one as easy and fun to tease
as a sister — and who else can be trusted
to be so forgiving?

*Laurie Harper*

If you don't understand how a woman could
both love her sister dearly and want to wring
her neck at the same time, you were
probably an only child.

*Linda Sunshine*

More than Santa Claus,
your sister knows when
you've been bad or good.

*Linda Sunshine*

One of the greatest
things in life is being able
to play the role
of a helping sister.

*Barbara Mandrell*

If you have a sister still living, hug her!

*Patti LaBelle*

Sometimes, the light at
the end of the tunnel
is your sister
with a flashlight.

*Karen Brown*

# Sources

If you enjoyed this book, you'll also enjoy other inspirational quotation books from WALNUT GROVE PRESS.

Other books by Angela Beasley Freeman include *Minutes from the Great Women's Coffee Club* and *100 Years of Women's Wisdom.*

For more information call 1-800-256-8584.